Contents

Milk

Milk comes from cows. It is sold in cartons and bottles.

Cows eat a lot of grass to help them make milk.

On Your Plate

Milk, Cheese and Eggs

Honor Head

FRANKLIN WATTS
LONDON • SYDNEY

This edition 2012

First published in 2008 by
Franklin Watts
338 Euston Road, London NW1 3BH

Franklin Watts Australia
Level 17/207 Kent St, Sydney, NSW 2000

Created by Honor Head and Jean Coppendale, Taglines
Design: Sumit Charles; Harleen Mehta, Q2A Media
Picture research: Shreya Sharma, Q2A Media

ISBN: 978 1 4451 0797 4

Dewey classification: 641.3'7

A CIP catalogue for this book is available from the British Library.

Picture credits
t=top b=bottom c=centre l=left r=right m=middle

Cover Images: Shutterstock and Istockphoto.
Photosky/ Dreamstime: 4, Julián Rovagnati/ Shutterstock: 5, Ene/ Shutterstock: 6, Marie C. Fields/ Shutterstock: 7, Spirita/ Istockphoto: 8, Cerlobea/ Dreamstime: 9, Thepalmer, Juanmonino/ Istockphoto: 10, Ivonnewierink/ Shutterstock: 11, Adlifemarketing/ Istockphoto: 12, Markstout/ Dreamstime: 13, Adlifemarketing/ Istockphoto: 14, Elkeflorida/ Istockphoto: 15, Stevenpepple/ Shutterstock: 16, Vangelis/ Shutterstock: 17, Harrisshiffman/ Shutterstock: 18, Ayeshawilson/ Shutterstock: 19, Joegough/ Shutterstock: 20, Pålespenolsen/ Shutterstock: 21.

Printed in China

Franklin Watts is a division of Hachette Children's Books,
an Hachette UK company.
www.hachette.co.uk

Milk makes your bones and teeth grow strong and healthy.

Try to drink some milk every day.

Milk foods

Foods such as butter, cheese, yogurt and cream are made from milk.

 Foods made from milk are called dairy foods.

Butter is spread on bread and toast. It is also used in cooking.

Butter melted on toast makes it tastier to eat.

Yogurt

Yogurt is thick and creamy. It is sold in cartons in lots of different flavours.

Yogurt is tasty and good for you.

Mix your favourite fruit with a bowl of plain yogurt.

Try yogurt as a topping on cereal or a dessert. You can use yogurt instead of cream.

Hard cheese

Cheeses such as Edam, Cheddar and Gouda are called hard cheeses.

Each hard cheese has a different taste.

Hard cheese is great in a sandwich or eaten on its own as a snack.

A cheese salad sandwich and an apple make a healthy lunch.

Soft cheese

Creamy cheese that is easy to spread is called soft cheese.

Soft cheese tastes good on crackers.

Cottage cheese is a soft cheese that is sold in a tub. You can eat it with salad, on a jacket potato or by itself.

Cottage cheese makes a delicious and healthy meal.

Cooking with cheese

Different cheeses are used to make savoury and sweet dishes.

Cheese is melted to make a sauce for broccoli and cauliflower.

Cheesecake is made with soft cheese mixed with sugar.

Cheesecake can be served with fruit sauce.

Eggs

Eggs are laid by female chickens called hens.

 Hens can lay brown or white eggs.

An egg has a shell outside. Inside is a yellow yolk and egg white.

Uncooked eggs are runny inside.

Cooking with eggs

Many foods have eggs in them. Eggs are used to make pasta, custard, cakes and puddings.

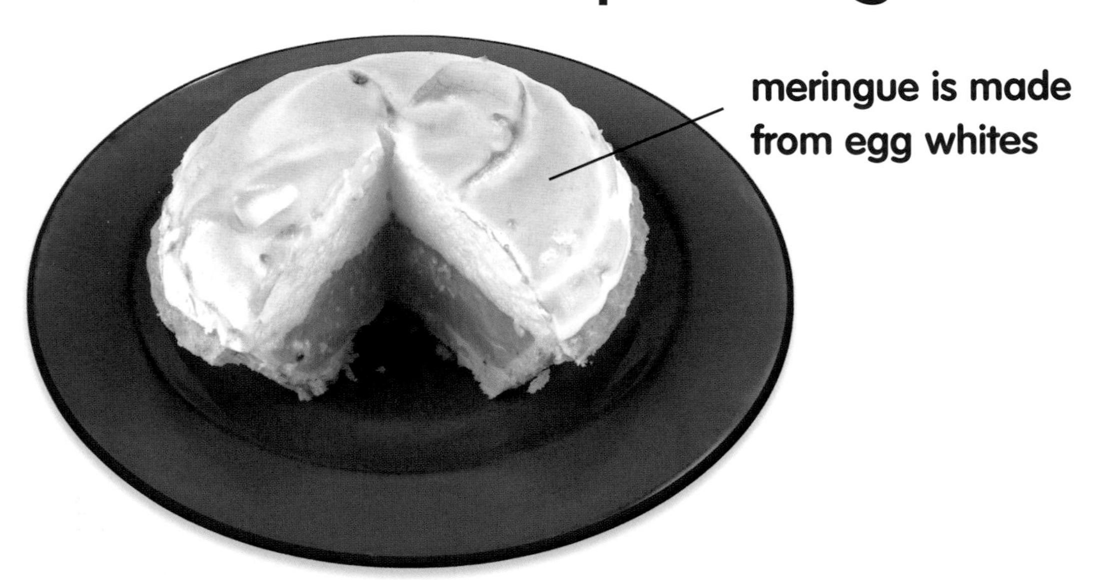

This lemon pudding has a meringue topping.

Salad with hard-boiled eggs is easy to make and very good for you.

When eggs are cooked in their shells in boiling water they become hard. These are called hard-boiled eggs.

Breakfast eggs

Lots of people have eggs for breakfast. Try them boiled, scrambled, fried or poached.

Scrambled eggs on toast makes a tasty breakfast.

Omelettes are delicious for breakfast or as a quick meal any time of day.

Have a ham or vegetable omelette for a filling meal.

Things to do

Cheesy choice

Can you name these cheeses? Which is cottage cheese? Which is Gouda? Which is Edam?

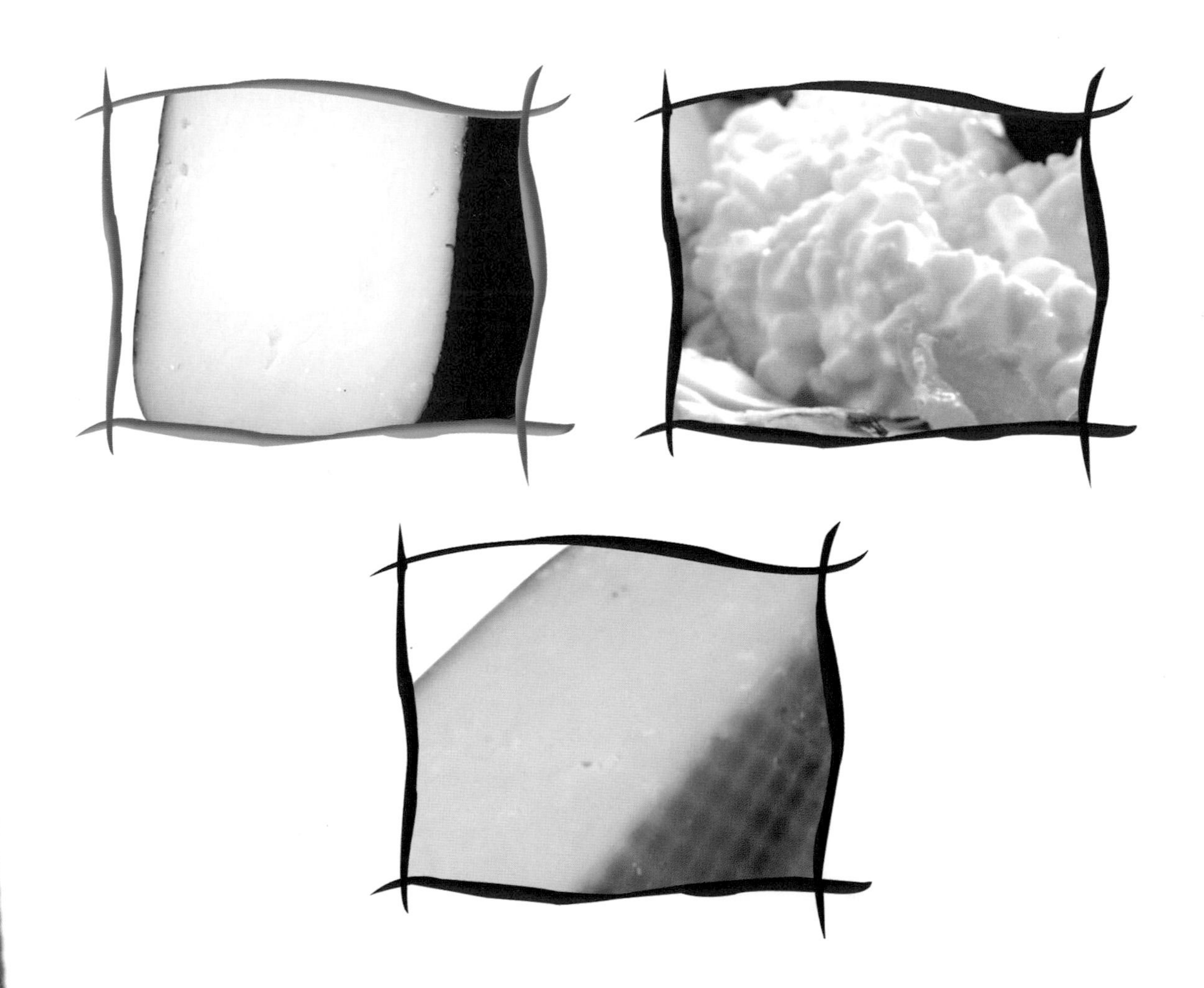

Eggscellent!

Can you match the two halves to find an omelette, scrambled egg on toast and a boiled egg salad?

Super sandwich

Which of these foods would make a tasty sandwich filling?

Glossary

dairy foods
These are any foods made from milk such as butter, cheese, yogurt and cream.

dessert
Another name for pudding.

poached
A way of cooking food, such as eggs without their shells, in boiling water.

savoury
A food that is not sweet.

Index